How to use this book

Matched to the National Curriculum, this Collins Year 6 Spelling workbook is designed to improve spelling skills.

Handy **tips** included throughout.

Questions split into three levels of difficulty – **Challenge 1**, **Challenge 2** and **Challenge 3** – to help progression.

Teaching notes to guide you through some of the key aspects of spelling.

Total marks boxes for recording progress and '**How am I doing?**' checks for self-evaluation.

Starter test recaps skills covered in Year 5.

Four **Progress tests** included throughout the book for ongoing assessment and monitoring progress.

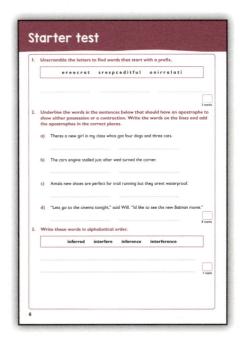

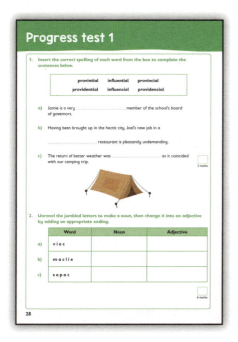

Answers provided for all the questions.

Contents

Practising spelling at home	4
Starter test	6
Endings which sound like **shus** spelt -cious	12
Endings which sound like **shus** spelt -tious	14
Endings which sound like **shul** spelt -cial and -tial	16
The endings -ant, -ance and -ancy	18
The endings -ent, -ence and -ency	20
The endings -able and -ible	22
The endings -ably and -ibly	24
Dictionary skills (1)	26
Progress test 1	28
The letter string 'ough'	32
Silent letters	34
Apostrophes for possession	36
Apostrophes for contraction	38
Using hyphens	40
Adding suffixes beginning with vowels to words ending in -fer	42
Dictionary skills (2)	44
Word games (1)	46
Progress test 2	48
Words with 'ei' and 'ie'	52
Adding the suffixes -ate, -ise and -ify to make verbs	54
Adding the suffix -en to make verbs	56
Homophones and near-homophones (1)	58
Homophones and near-homophones (2)	60

Words with unspoken sounds and syllables	62
Dictionary skills (3)	64
Word games (2)	66
Progress test 3	**68**
Prefixes	72
Latin and Greek prefixes	74
Words from other languages	76
Tricky plurals	78
Tricky words (1)	80
Tricky words (2)	82
Dictionary skills (4)	84
Word games (3)	86
Progress test 4	**88**
Answers	92

Acknowledgements

The author and publisher are grateful to the copyright holders for permission to use quoted materials and images. All illustrations and images are ©Shutterstock.com and ©HarperCollinsPublishers Ltd.

The Iron Man by Ted Hughes © Faber and Faber Ltd.

Published by Collins
An imprint of HarperCollinsPublishers
1 London Bridge Street
London SE1 9GF

HarperCollinsPublishers
Macken House, 39/40 Mayor Street Upper,
Dublin 1, D01 C9W8, Ireland

© HarperCollinsPublishers Limited 2024

ISBN 978-0-00-862713-3

First published 2024

10 9 8 7 6 5 4 3 2

British Library Cataloguing in Publication Data.

A CIP record of this book is available from the British Library.

Publisher: Jennifer Hall
Author: Shelley Welsh
Project Leaders: Richard Toms and Shelley Teasdale
Editorial: Fiona Watson
Cover Design: Sarah Duxbury
Inside Concept Design and Page Layout: Ian Wrigley
Production: Bethany Brohm
Printed in India by Multivista Global Pvt. Ltd.

MIX
Paper | Supporting responsible forestry
FSC™ C007454

This book is produced from independently certified FSC™ paper to ensure responsible forest management.

For more information visit: www.harpercollins.co.uk/green

Practising spelling at home

In Year 6, children's spelling skills and physical handwriting skills continue to develop. As they read longer, more complex texts and become increasingly independent readers, they will be exposed to a wider range of vocabulary and more challenging spellings.

Having good spelling skills helps children write more fluently as they do not need to spend too long considering how each word is spelt. In turn, they will have the confidence to make more adventurous vocabulary choices and to develop their reading skills in using a dictionary to check for spelling accuracy and word meaning.

Supporting your child

When supporting your child at home, draw their attention to spelling patterns. These might be sound or letter patterns, grammar patterns or word families. It is important to remember that although there are many spelling rules, there are also many words that are exceptions to any obvious rule or pattern. These words just have to be learned.

Your child's vocabulary can be extended by actively engaging in conversation with you and other adults, and by reading a range of genres independently. Encourage your child to be curious about vocabulary, its meaning and how it is spelt. Discussing what your child has been reading, watching on television or listening to on the radio or in podcasts will help develop their vocabulary and their understanding of grammar, as well as their ability to access other areas of the curriculum.

There are many ways that your child can practise spelling at home, independently and with support, and there are a range of practical activities that you might do with your child.

Look, cover, write, check

Look, cover, write, check is a strategy taught in schools which can also be used at home. Write the words your child is learning in the first column of a three- or four-column table. Ask your child to look at the spelling, cover it, write the spelling in the next column then uncover the original spelling to check if they have got it right. The additional blank columns can be used for corrections or extra practice.

Flash cards

Create a double set of the words your child finds tricky to spell. They pick up two cards at a time until they find a pair. Ask them to spell the word out to you verbally.

Word searches and crossword puzzles

There are internet sites for both these activities, as well as many printed books and magazines.

Tic Tac Toe

Create a 'noughts and crosses' grid and provide your child and another player with a face-down pile of the words they are learning and a different colour marker for each player. Players take it in turns to choose a spelling from the pile, read it, memorise the spelling, then write it in one of the grid spaces. The winner is the first to get three-in-a-row correctly spelt words.

Computer or tablet

Give your child the opportunity to type the words they are learning and to experiment with text fonts, sizes and colours.

Creating a good learning environment

As children learn best when they do not feel under pressure, distracted or tired, it is important that your child is:

- positive
- comfortable about making mistakes
- not rushed
- in a quiet, calm working place
- encouraged to check their work.

The importance of reading

Finally, encourage your child to read, read, read! Not only does reading improve their spelling and vocabulary, it stimulates their imagination and is a relaxing pastime in the midst of busy lives too often dominated by screens. Reading is more than just a skill and the impact of *reading for pleasure* should never be underestimated.

Starter test

1. **Unscramble the letters to find words that start with a prefix.**

   | ereecrat   srespceditful   onirralati |

   ....

   3 marks

2. **Underline the words in the sentences below that should have an apostrophe to show either possession or a contraction. Write the words on the lines and add the apostrophes in the correct places.**

   a) Theres a new girl in my class whos got four dogs and three cats.

   ....

   b) The cars engine stalled just after wed turned the corner.

   ....

   c) Amals new shoes are perfect for trail running but they arent waterproof.

   ....

   d) "Lets go to the cinema tonight," said Will. "Id like to see the new *Batman* movie."

   ....

   8 marks

3. **Write these words in alphabetical order.**

   | inferred   interfere   inference   interference |

   ....

   ....

   1 mark

4. **Choose the correct spelling of the words in bold. Write the correct word on the line below each sentence.**

a) Martha thought the new restaurant was very **pretencious / pretentious**.

....

b) Although disappointed, Nina accepted the runner-up prize **graciously / gratiously**.

....

c) Rumours of the building of a new leisure centre in our town turned out to be **fictitious / ficticious**.

....

3 marks

5. **Write the word that is missing its silent letter on the line below each sentence.**

a) Since his accident, Uwe struggles to fasen his buttons.

....

b) My cousin Alba, whom I'd not seen for years, is a famous playright.

....

c) Leo is undoutedly the most talented gymnast in our school.

....

3 marks

6. **The words below have a shun sound at the end but they have been spelt incorrectly. Write the correct spellings on the lines.**

   a)   intenshun   ....

   b)   processhun   ....

   c)   decepshun   ....

   d)   electrishun   ....

7. **Write the homophones that are the answers to these clues.**

   a)   A cat's or a dog's feet

        ....

   b)   To stop for a short period

        ....

   c)   An adjective meaning very small

        ....

   d)   A sixtieth of an hour

        ....

   e)   A long-eared mammal that looks like a large rabbit

        ....

   f)   The thread-like structures that grow out of the skin of a person or animal

        ....

8. **Add a prefix to each of the following words to complete the sentences.**

| heard   regular   practical |

a) Grandpa has been diagnosed with an ....
   heartbeat.

b) Issey wrote the wrong word as she ....
   what Finn told her.

c) Once the sun came out, my warm fleece was quite

   .... for my walk.

3 marks

9. **Use the clues to find words which end with a k sound or a hard g sound.**

a) I am a group of teams that play the same sport. I am of French origin and I
   end with a hard **g** sound.

   I am a ....

b) I am an adjective meaning one of a kind and I end with a **k** sound .

   I am ....

c) I am an old, valuable and often rare object and I end with a **k** sound.

   I am an ....

3 marks

10. **Add a prefix to each of these words.**

a) .... c o n t i n u e

b) .... g r a p h

c) .... w a y

d) .... d o t e

4 marks

11. Find the words in the passage below that have an apostrophe and write them in the correct column in the table.

Sitting in the back of Dad's car, Erin couldn't remember whether she'd packed her diary. She intended to write in it every day of this year's holiday in Gran's cottage by the sea. It was where she recorded her innermost thoughts and dreams. A bit like Anne Frank's diary, which Anne called 'Kitty', Erin felt the small, blue book covered in butterflies was her friend, someone who'd listen. Someone who didn't judge her.

Apostrophe to show a contraction	Apostrophe to show possession

8 marks

12. Add the suffix -ation to the following verbs to make nouns.

a) initiate ....

b) condemn ....

c) designate ....

d) inspire ....

4 marks

13. **Add the suffix -ed to each verb below then complete the sentences.**

| prefer | deny | bury | permit |

a) Nigel .... knocking over the vase of beautiful flowers.

b) Pat said she .... the first Harry Potter book out of the three she had read.

c) Visitors are not .... to walk on the grass.

d) Rafa, our dog, ... his bone behind the garden shed.

4 marks

Total: _____ / 54 marks

Endings which sound like shus spelt -cious

Challenge 1

1 Say these words out loud. Write the word, marking the syllable breaks with a vertical line. Then write the word again.

One has been done for you.

precocious   *pre | co | cious*   *precocious*

a) tenacious   ....

b) spacious   ....

c) luscious   ....

6 marks

2 Match the words from Question 1 to their definitions in the table, including the word in the example. Use your dictionary to help you if you need to.

Definition	Word
Describes a place that is large in size	a)
Describes food that is juicy and good to eat	b)
Describes someone who is very determined	c)
Describes a clever and mature child	d)

4 marks

Challenge 2

1 Write a sentence for each word in Challenge 1.

a) ....

b) ....

c) ....

d) ....

8 marks

Challenge 3

Teaching note

A synonym is a word that has the same or a similar meaning as another word. An antonym is a word that has an opposite meaning to another word.

1 Use a thesaurus to find a synonym and an antonym for each word in the middle of the table below.

	Synonym	Word	Antonym
a)		conscious	
b)		avaricious	
c)		precious	
d)		vivacious	
e)		malicious	

10 marks

Total: _____ / 28 marks

😐 **Had a go** ☐   🙂 **Getting there** ☐   😃 **Got it!** ☐

Endings which sound like shus spelt -tious

If a related word ends in -tion, the **shus** sound is usually spelt -tious. For example, infection → infectious. Other words don't follow a spelling rule – they just have to be learned.

Challenge 1

1 Complete the sentences with the appropriate form of the words below.

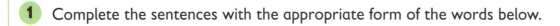

repetition   nutrition   fiction   contend

a) The teacher said my essay was too long-winded and very

....

b) Gaynor refused to eat ....
food such as fruit and vegetables.

c) The director made it clear that the characters in the film were

completely ....

d) The proposed building of the new leisure centre is a

.... issue with villagers.

4 marks

Challenge 2

1 Match the words to their definitions below.

| surreptitious | flirtatious |
| conscientious | ostentatious |

Definition	Word
The playful behaviour from someone when they are attracted to a person	a)
Something that is expensive and intended to impress	b)
An action that is done secretly	c)
Someone who is very careful to do their work properly	d)

4 marks

Challenge 3

1 Select the correct word from the box to complete the sentences below.
Use your dictionary to help you if you need to.

| scrumptious | pretentious |
| fractious | superstitious |

a) The new hotel is full of ill-mannered, ... people.

b) When my baby sisters are tired, they become very ....

c) Perry, who is very ...., refuses to walk under a ladder.

d) Dessert was a delightful spread of the most .... cupcakes, fruit tarts and puddings.

4 marks

Total: _____ / 12 marks

 Had a go Getting there Got it!

Endings which sound like shul spelt -cial and -tial

The ending -cial is common after a vowel and the ending -tial is common after a consonant. For example, facial and partial.

Challenge 1

1 Change these nouns into adjectives.

a) sacrifice ....

b) president ....

c) torrent ....

d) prejudice ....

4 marks

2 Write a sentence for each word you created in Question 1.

a) ....

b) ....

c) ....

d) ....

8 marks

Challenge 2

1 Complete each sentence with an appropriate word from the box below.

insubstantial   judicial   preferential   superficial

a) I thought the book's main character lacked depth; in fact, she was completely

....

b) It was decided to settle the issue in court with a

.... inquiry.

c) Thomas's shelter on the wild camping trip was a flimsy,

.... tent.

d) The princess, wishing to blend in with the rest of us, did not want

.... treatment.

4 marks

Challenge 3

1 Add either -cial or -tial to the words in the box then write a definition for each. Use your dictionary to help you if you need to.

confidence	potent	consequence

a) ....

b) ....

c) ....

6 marks

2 How are the words 'financial' and 'spatial' exceptions to the spelling rule?

....

....

2 marks

Total: _____ / 24 marks

 Had a go   **Getting there**   **Got it!**

The endings -ant, -ance and -ancy

Teaching note

If there is a related word with an **ah** or an **ay** sound in the penultimate syllable, use -ant, -ance or -ancy. Words with an -ation ending are often a clue. For example, observation → observ**ant**. However, there are many words where the spelling guidance does not help. They just have to be learned!

Challenge 1

Teaching note

An abstract noun denotes an idea, quality or state rather than a concrete object. For example, courage (abstract) vs house (concrete).

1 Change each abstract noun into a concrete noun with the same root but ending in -ant.

a) participation   ....

b) consultation   ....

c) migration   ....

d) contamination   ....

4 marks

Challenge 2

1 Unscramble the letters to find words that end in -ant, -ance and -ancy.

erencleva   cnscyuoltan

rantdia   omcplicean

....

....

4 marks

Challenge 3

1 Use the clues to complete the crossword.

Across

6. The importance of something (noun)
8. Present in large quantities (adjective)

Down

1. The practice of keeping financial accounts (noun)
2. Someone who believes they can communicate with the dead (noun and adjective)
3. Loyalty to someone or something (noun)
4. The careful observation of someone (noun)
5. Opposed to something (adjective)
7. Stylish in an exciting way (adjective)

8 marks

Total: _____ / 16 marks

The endings -ent, -ence and -ency

Challenge 1

1 Change these adjectives into nouns.

a) efficient ....

b) consequent ....

c) convenient ....

d) permanent ....

e) persistent ....

f) turbulent ....

6 marks

Challenge 2

1 Ciara has spelt four of her homework spellings incorrectly. Write her corrections on the lines. Use a dictionary to help you.

correspondant	expectant
frequency	existance
hesitant	precedant
equivalent	succulant

4 marks

Challenge 3

1 Match the words below to their definitions then write a sentence containing each word.

| resplendent | congruent | proficiency |

a) ....

Definition: In agreement with something else

Sentence: ....

....

b) ....

Definition: An ability or skill in something

Sentence: ....

....

c) ....

Definition: Impressive or expensive-looking

Sentence: ....

....

9 marks

Total: _____ / 19 marks

The endings -able and -ible

Challenge 1

1 The missing words in the sentences below all end with -able or -ible. Each word starts with a negative prefix. Use the clues to help you complete the words.

a) Isla's puppy has so much energy; he is completely

un .... t .... p .... when he starts charging around!

Clue: cannot be stopped

b) Markus denied that his brother had behaved in a

dis .... put .... way.

Clue: not honest

c) It is almost in .... omp .... hens .... to think that our school is closing down next year.

Clue: impossible to understand

3 marks

Challenge 2

1 Unscramble the letters to complete the words ending in -able or -ible.

a) a l e s u r a b e p l

pl...

b) n f a l e l l i i b

inf...

c) c e e t i f i r a b l

cert..

3 marks

Teaching note

If the -able ending is added to a word ending in -ce or -ge, the 'e' after the 'c' or 'g' must be kept to keep their sounds soft.

Challenge 3

1 Change the words below into adjectives by adding an appropriate suffix.

| recharge | salvage | trace |

....

3 marks

2 Use the words you made in Question 1 to complete the following sentences.

a) Unfortunately, the shipwrecked boat was not ....

b) Luckily, Jamil's torch uses .... batteries.

c) The detective said the fingerprints were .... to a well-known criminal.

3 marks

Total: _____ / 12 marks

😐 **Had a go** ☐   🙂 **Getting there** ☐   😄 **Got it!** ☐

23

The endings -ably and -ibly

Challenge 1

1   Complete the words in the passage by adding the endings -ably or -ibly.

Bruce was vis............... delighted that his team lost the match.

It turned out that he had been treated abomin............... by the

coach when he had played in goal many years before.

However, argu............... Bruce may have deserved some criticism

as he often missed training sessions or turned up irrespons...............

late for matches.

4 marks

Challenge 2

1   Unscramble the letters to complete the words ending in -ably or -ibly.

a)   l g i l e b y   l e ....

b)   i r u n e y s d b a l   u n d e s ....

c)   f s i b l y e a   f e a ....

d)   b i n s r e y p a a l   i n s e ....

4 marks

Challenge 3

1 Find the seven words in the passage that have been spelt incorrectly. Write the correct spellings on the lines.

> Justine has an envyably lavish lifestyle but that wasn't always the case. When she was young, she and her brothers were forcably taken from their home and spent a few months living on a farm where they were unjustifibly treated in an inexplicibly cruel way. Fortunately, they were rescued by the incredably kind Mr and Mrs Smith and now, irreversably plump and terrably smug, they spend their days being fed sardines and fresh cream. *Miaow!*

....

....

....

....   7 marks

2 Write a sentence containing two of the words from Question 1.

....

....

2 marks

Total: _____ / 17 marks

Dictionary skills (1)

Challenge 1

1 Use your dictionary to find a verb made from each noun below. Write the verbs on the lines.

character	opposition	repetition	deception

....

....

4 marks

Challenge 2

1 Write a word that comes alphabetically between the pairs of words below.

a) symbol .... symptom .... system

b) zap .... zip .... zodiac

c) incidental .... incisor .... income

d) mountain .... mouse .... mouth

8 marks

1 Make a silly sentence using four words chosen from the following places in your dictionary. You can make your sentence as silly as you like!

First word: page 24, second column

Second word: page 56, first column

Third word: page 87, second column

Fourth word: page 154, first column

....

....

....

2 marks

2 Use your dictionary to find the word class and definition of each word below.

| boor | modify | debris | circumspect |

Word	Class	Definition

8 marks

Total: _____ / 22 marks

 Had a go   Getting there   Got it!

Progress test 1

1. Insert the correct spelling of each word from the box to complete the sentences below.

provintial	influential	provincial
providential	influencial	providencial

   a) Jamie is a very .... member of the school's board of governors.

   b) Having been brought up in the hectic city, Joel's new job in a

   .... restaurant is pleasantly undemanding.

   c) The return of better weather was .... as it coincided with our camping trip.

   3 marks

2. Unravel the jumbled letters to make a noun, then change it into an adjective by adding an appropriate ending.

	Word	Noun	Adjective
a)	v i e c		
b)	m a c l i e		
c)	s e p a c		

   6 marks

3. **Change the adjectives below into nouns then complete the sentences.**

impudent	resurgent	diligent	incompetent

....

....

a) The leaking tap was down to Maya's .... as a lazy and reluctant plumber.

b) As a result of the manager's ...., I shall never return to that shop!

c) Petra's hard work and .... was rewarded with a pay rise and promotion.

d) The recent .... of fifties music has pleased my grandparents.

4 marks

4. **Use a dictionary to find two different definitions for 'match' as a noun and two different definitions for 'match' as a verb.**

Noun (1)	
Noun (2)	
Verb (1)	
Verb (2)	

4 marks

29

5. **Match these adjectives to their definitions, then write a sentence containing each one.**

> crucial   antisocial   impartial

a) ....

Definition: Extremely important

Sentence: ....

....

b) ....

Definition: Not directly involved so able to give a fair opinion

Sentence: ....

....

c) ....

Definition: Unwilling to meet and be friendly with other people

Sentence: ....

....

9 marks

6. Find eight words in the word search that end in -able or -ably and write them on the lines below.

d	r	e	f	e	r	e	n	c	e	d	u	b
i	n	c	o	n	c	e	i	v	a	b	l	y
s	i	e	r	h	f	i	q	u	e	f	j	t
t	n	i	m	f	p	r	q	n	c	e	k	y
i	q	n	i	n	c	u	r	a	b	l	e	e
n	u	e	d	q	r	e	u	w	q	r	n	r
g	e	d	a	f	r	x	e	n	m	e	v	w
u	s	s	b	e	d	e	f	w	r	d	j	q
i	t	i	l	q	e	r	r	e	d	w	n	a
s	i	n	e	x	p	l	i	c	a	b	l	y
h	o	r	t	y	w	w	y	q	u	b	m	n
a	n	e	g	o	t	i	a	b	l	e	v	e
b	a	q	w	e	r	t	y	u	k	m	b	v
l	b	e	l	i	e	v	a	b	l	y	v	n
e	l	v	c	x	z	z	w	e	a	a	c	k
x	y	w	w	b	m	l	u	h	f	h	f	k

....

....

....

....

8 marks

Total: _____ / 34 marks

The letter string 'ough'

Challenge 1

1 Solve the clues to write the words that contain the letter string 'ough'.

a) I am a long, narrow container from which farm animals eat or drink.

t ....

b) I am a large farming tool with sharp blades used for turning soil over.

p ....

c) I am the past tense of the verb bring.

....

d) You might do this to clear your throat, particularly when you're ill.

....

4 marks

Challenge 2

1 The words below have been spelt as they sound but they should all contain the letter string 'ough'. Write them correctly, grouping them according to the sound 'ough' makes in each case.

| enuff | althow | bawt | bow | tuff | coff | brawt |
| dow | thawt | plow | fawt | awt | troff | thow |

14 marks

1 Unscramble the two words below which contain the letter string 'ough', then write a sentence for each.

> **r u h l t o y o g h   o r o h u b g**

....

a) ....

....

b) ....

....

6 marks

Total: _____ / 24 marks

Silent letters

Challenge 1

1 The following words have been spelt without their silent letters. Rewrite them correctly on the lines.

a) veemently ....

b) undoutedly ....

c) narled ....

d) nowledgeably ....

e) wite ....

f) rinoceros ....

6 marks

Challenge 2

1 Write the answers to the definitions on the lines next to each.

    a)   To fit something tightly somewhere   w ....

    b)   The yellow part of an egg   y ....

    c)   Describes something filled with air   p ....

3 marks

Challenge 3

1 Find the fourteen words in the passage that are missing their silent letters. Write them on the lines below.

> Tania waked camly through the huge casle door, then tensed her musles; she looked in awe at the colums which held up the roof. At the end of a long aile, a narled and twisted old man was singing a well-nown hym. A gost-like figure approached her and asked, "Are you in receit of the magic potion?" "Yes," Tanya ansered, agast at the thout of relinquishing it. "Here it is."

....

....

....

....

....

....

....

14 marks

Total: _____ / 23 marks

😐 **Had a go** ☐   🙂 **Getting there** ☐   😄 **Got it!** ☐

Apostrophes for possession

Teaching note

To show possession of a singular noun, an apostrophe is placed after the final letter followed by an 's'. For example, the flower's petals. For plural nouns ending in 's', the apostrophe is placed after the 's'. For example, the flowers' petals.

Challenge 1

1 Select the word that has been written correctly from the words in bold.
Write the correct word on the line.

a) The **girls' / girl's** hockey sticks were left on the pitch after they had won the game.

....

b) Our teaching **staffs' / staff's** night out is always held in the pizza restaurant.

....

c) The **bee's / bees'** wings became dusty with pollen as it busied itself around the flowers.

....

d) Mum had to alter the **dress's / dresses'** length as it was too long.

....

4 marks

Teaching note

For singular nouns ending in 'ss', the apostrophe is placed after the final 's' and is followed by another 's'. For example, the waitress's apron. For plural nouns ending in 'ss', where 'es' is added to form the plural, the apostrophe comes after the final 's'. For example, the waitresses' aprons. For irregular plurals, the apostrophe is placed after the final letter and before the letter 's'. For example, the men's bikes.

Challenge 2

1 The words in bold in each sentence below are missing their apostrophes. Write the words on the lines and insert the apostrophes, plus the missing 's' if needed.

a) Renee could hear the **bus** brakes screeching as it rounded the corner.

....

b) The **Smiths** new dog has escaped from their garden yet again.

....

c) Both our **bosses** fancy new cars have built-in sat-nav and retractable roofs.

....

d) The **childrens** tickets were checked before they were ushered into the cinema.

....

4 marks

Challenge 3

1 Write the six words that are missing their possessive apostrophes on the lines below and insert the missing apostrophes.

Kyles bike is from Bills Bicycles, the towns only cycle shop which is located next to Dads chemist at the end of a row of shops. Its frame is blue and silver and there are 12 gears. Its saddle contains gel pads that provide extra comfort on long trips such as this weekends 50 km ride, which he is doing to raise money for the Trillbury Dogs Home charity.

....

....

6 marks

Total: _____ / 14 marks

😐 **Had a go** ☐   🙂 **Getting there** ☐   😃 **Got it!** ☐

Apostrophes for contraction

Challenge 1

1. Find the words in the text messages that could be written as contractions rather than in their full forms. Write the contracted forms.

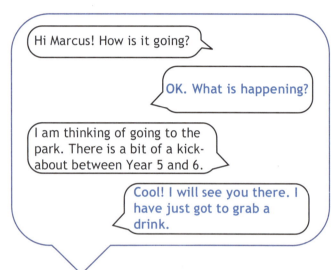

Hi Marcus! How is it going?

OK. What is happening?

I am thinking of going to the park. There is a bit of a kick-about between Year 5 and 6.

Cool! I will see you there. I have just got to grab a drink.

6 marks

Challenge 2

1. Write the full forms of these words where a letter or letters have been dropped by the speaker.

goin'	wishin'	'cause	'avin'
....	....	....	....

4 marks

Challenge 3

1 Fred has written an email to the headteacher using the voice record facility on his phone. His teacher has explained that it needs to be more formal. Write the full forms of the words he has written as contractions on the lines below.

Mrs McGuire
Prancington Primary School
PP1 2PP

Dear Mrs McGuire,

D'you remember when you said in assembly that you'd like us all to tell you if we've got any ideas to improve the school? Well, that's why I'm writing!

I'd love it if we didn't have to do any homework. It's a nightmare havin' to do it at weekends, especially when I've got better things to do. You'd think the board of governors would want its kids to be happy.

Another thing is our uniform – we're always being laughed at by the kids from the secondary school. They've got a cool uniform and can wear any coat they like.
Can we at least have a committee to discuss it? I'd definitely volunteer to be on it.

Let's get together when you've got some spare time.

Fred

....

....

....

....

....

16 marks

Total: _____ / 26 marks

 Had a go ☐   **Getting there** ☐   **Got it!** ☐

Using hyphens

Teaching note

Hyphens can be used to join prefixes to words and to form compound words and adjectives. For example, thick-set. Sometimes, a hyphen is needed to avoid ambiguity. For example, re-cover versus recover. And sometimes it is needed because the prefix ends in a vowel and the word begins with a vowel. For example, re-enter.

Challenge 1

1 The hyphenated compound words in the sentences below have been mis-matched. Write the sentences correctly on the lines.

Stacey is wearing a **light-fetched** silk scarf.

....

There were **twenty-new** children on the bus this morning.

....

Tamara felt the story was a little **far-three**.

....

Today I rode my **brand-blue** bike to the park.

....

4 marks

2 Explain the difference in meaning between the two sentences below.

We saw a man eating shark today.

We saw a man-eating shark today.

....

....

2 marks

Challenge 2

1 Use a hyphen to join a prefix to a word, then write the words on the lines below.

de   re   co   self

control   establish   author   escalate

....

....

4 marks

Challenge 3

1 Write a definition for each word below. Use your dictionary to help you.

Word	Definition
re-count	a)
recount	b)
re-form	c)
reform	d)

4 marks

Total: _____ / 14 marks

Adding suffixes beginning with vowels to words ending in -fer

Teaching note

When adding a suffix beginning with a vowel to a word ending in -fer, the 'r' is doubled if the syllable -fer is still stressed after the suffix is added. If the syllable -fer is unstressed, the 'r' is not doubled.

Challenge 1

1   Write the number of 'r's there would be in each word after adding the suffix -ed.

a)   buffer ☐

b)   confer ☐

c)   defer ☐

d)   refer ☐

☐ 4 marks

Challenge 2

1   Complete the table by adding the suffixes -er, -ed and -ing to the verbs. Be careful – not all the suffixes can be added to all the words! Write the words, where applicable, in the correct area of the table.

Verb	-er	-ed	-ing
transfer			
suffer			
pilfer			
infer			

☐ 10 marks

Challenge 3

1 Use the clues to complete the crossword.

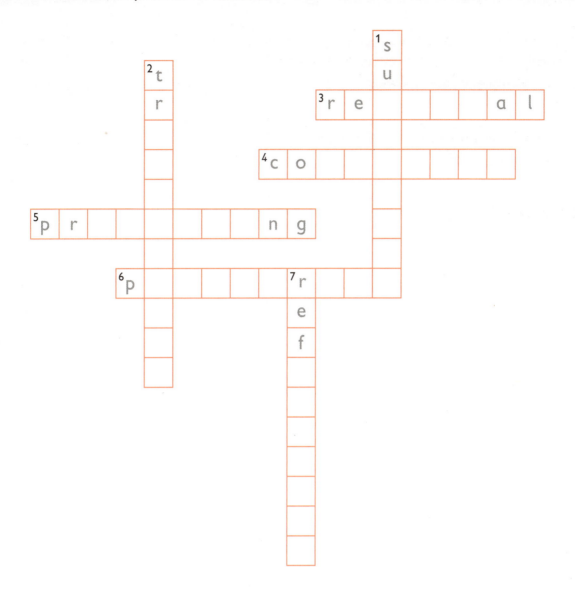

Across

3. The act of sending someone to a person or authority such as a doctor
4. Discussed with someone so a decision can be made
5. Holding something towards someone so that it can be taken
6. Liking someone or something better than another

Down

1. Feeling pain in your body or mind
2. Moved from one place to another
7. A public vote or ballot

7 marks

Total: _____ / 21 marks

Dictionary skills (2)

Challenge 1

1 Use a thesaurus to find one synonym for each word below. Write the synonym on the line.

a) culprit ....

b) hectic ....

c) inevitable ....

d) ploy ....

4 marks

2 Write these words in alphabetical order.

| programme | profound | profession | prophecy |

....

....

....

....

1 mark

44

Challenge 2

1 Use a thesaurus to find an antonym for each word below.

a) compress ....

b) disperse ....

c) robust ....

d) lenient ....

Challenge 3

1 Use your dictionary to help you find the word class of the words in bold in the passage below.

> An eye! There it was, **blinking** at them speechlessly beside a black and white **pebble**. The seeing hand **fitted** the eye to the **blind** hand and now both hands could see. They went running among the rocks. Soon they found a leg. They jumped on top of the leg and the leg went **hopping** over the rocks with the arm swinging from the hand that clung to the top of the leg.
>
> from *The Iron Man* by Ted Hughes

Word	Word class

Total: _____ / 14 marks

Word games (1)

Challenge 1

1 Find the word in bold that has a similar meaning to both of the pairs of words in the brackets.

a) (difficult, challenging)   (solid, firm)

   stiff   **hard**   **rigid**   **static**   **awkward**

   ....

b) (refuge, sanctuary)   (protect, safeguard)

   asylum   **guard**   **haven**   **lodge**   **shelter**

   ....

c) (enclosure, fold)   (biro, felt-tip)

   pen   **brush**   **sheep**   **paper**   **sign**

   ....

d) (purpose, use)   (party, event)

   social   **invite**   **ball**   **function**   **do**

   ....

4 marks

Challenge 2

1 Rearrange the jumbled letters in each word written in bold to spell a word that completes the sentence. Write the word on the line.

a) I misread the **n u c i s n s t r t i o** and screwed the table legs on upside down.

   ....

b) Greta likes top **i q t y u a l** clothes which are expensive.

....

c) Bethan **d i o v c d e r e s** that she had a distant cousin whom she had never met.

....

d) Han is **i e d l n s c e** to drive the farmer's tractor.

....

4 marks

Challenge 3

1 Write the word that completes a third pair of words using the same pattern as the first two pairs.

a) bind band   hind hand   wind   ....

b) cabbage bag   luggage gag   sitting   ....

c) address sad   entreat ten   anthem   ....

d) grass rag   tears eat   swarm   ....

4 marks

Total: _____ / 12 marks

 Had a go ☐   **Getting there** ☐   😃 **Got it!** ☐

Progress test 2

1. **The words below have been spelt as they sound. Correct their spelling and add them to the sentences.**

fasinated	sucumed	colown	needed

a) Gerry .... the dough for about ten minutes.

b) Paul bought his favourite .... in the duty-free shop.

c) Penny was .... by the peacocks' brightly coloured tails.

d) Bridgit .... to a third helping of ice cream.

4 marks

2. **Solve the clues to complete the grid with words that have an 'ough' letter string.**

a) to do something carefully and completely

b) a town or district with its own council

c) a large branch of a tree

d) past tense of the verb 'fight'

a)	t						
b)	b						
c)	b						
d)	f						

4 marks

3. Use a thesaurus to find a synonym and an antonym for each word in the middle column of the table.

Synonym	Word	Antonym
	dominant	
	resplendent	
	compliant	
	precedent	

8 marks

4. Two apostrophes in each sentence are missing. Write the words on the lines and add the apostrophes in the correct places.

a)   The journalists excellent articles gained him two prizes at the awards ceremony in Londons five-star Hillcrest Hotel.

....

b)   Two ladies bikes have been found abandoned in the towns playing fields according to the notices in the local shops.

....

c)   Gunther was thrilled that his dads cake, which was decorated with strawberries and raspberry jam, won first prize at the farmers fair.

....

6 marks

5. The hyphens are missing from two pairs or groups of words in the sentences below. Rewrite the words on the lines and add the hyphens.

a) Sid is a fair skinned, blond haired man who burns easily on hot summer days.

....

b) The jumble sale was a bit of a disorganised free for all and we came back empty handed.

....

c) Kevin, Tamsin's twelve year old brother, is a know it all, according to Lin.

....

6 marks

6. Select the correctly spelt words in the box and write them in the sentences below.

transfered	transferred	bufferring
buffering	defered	deferred

a) May's mum is being .... from the Edinburgh office to the head office in Manchester.

b) Billie was exasperated watching the tennis because the picture kept

.... for most of the match.

c) The meeting has been .... until more people are able to attend.

3 marks

50

7. There are two different meanings and pronunciations for the words 'produce' and 'permit'. Write the two different meanings and the associated word class.

Word	Meanings	Class
produce		
produce		
permit		
permit		

8. Write the **12** contractions that are missing their apostrophes on the lines below.

Hi Cassie!

Cant believe Im actually here in New York! Its absolutely AMAZING! I know youd love it, especially the Statue of Liberty. Ive taken LOADS of pics which Ill show you when I get back. Mums taking me to the Rockefeller Center later whichll be SO cool! Havent seen anyone famous YET but watch this space …
Our hotels got a great view – were on the top floor. Gotta go. Hope youre OK.

Love Millie x

....

....

....

....

Total: _____ / 51 marks

Words with 'ei' and 'ie'

Challenge 1

1 Unscramble the letters to find words with an 'ei' spelling and an **ee** sound that is *not* preceded by the letter 'c'.

r p o n t e i   d e i r w   z e i e s   c a f n e f e i

....

....

4 marks

2 Write a sentence that contains one of the words from Question 1.

....

2 marks

3 Unscramble the letters to find words with an 'ei' spelling and **ee** sound that *is* preceded by the letter 'c'.

c o n t e e d c i   n c e c o i v e   e d i v c e e   r i e c v e e

....

....

4 marks

Challenge 2

1 Solve the clues to find words with an **ee** sound spelt 'ie'.

a) A minister in a church.

p ....

b) Someone who steals something from someone.

t ....

c) An adjective to describe something that only lasts a short time.

b ....

d) A feeling of certainty that something exists or is true.

b ....

4 marks

Tip   Some words *do* have an 'ie' spelling after the letter 'c'. For example, glacier.

Challenge 3

1 Find the nine words in the passage that have been spelt incorrectly. Write the correct spellings on the lines.

José went to the council breifing about the discovery of anceint ruins in the feild outside his village. A peice of clay, seemingly part of an urn, was the first item yeilded by the site. Dr Dishoom, a local sceintist, said he beleived it may have belonged to a pre-Christian community. José siezed the opportunity to ask him if it might be connected to a sheild he had found there the week before.

....

....

....

9 marks

Total: _____ / 23 marks

☺ **Had a go** ☐   ☺ **Getting there** ☐   ☺ **Got it!** ☐

53

Adding the suffixes -ate, -ise and -ify to make verbs

The suffixes -ate, -ise and -ify can be used to create verbs. Sometimes these refer to making something or someone different in some way. For example, solid → solidify: to make solid. When adding these suffixes to words ending in 'e', the 'e' is dropped. For example, false → falsify. When adding them to words ending in 'y', the 'y' is dropped or changed to 'i'. For example, beauty → beautify, luxury → luxuriate.

Challenge 1

1 Add the suffix -ate, -ise or -ify to each of the following words.

a) vaccine ....

b) agony ....

c) diverse ....

d) simple ....

e) valid ....

f) equal ....

6 marks

Challenge 2

1 Each of the following sentences is missing a verb. Add the suffixes -ate, -ise or -ify to each of the following words and add them to the correct sentence. You may need to make further spelling changes.

| note | hospital | fossil | glory | captive | hyphen |

a) Ivor was .... by the region's natural beauty.

b) Tilly's grandpa had to be .... after his bad fall.

c) The old soldier said that war should never be ....

d) We have been learning how to .... compound adjectives.

e) The geologist found an egg that had been ....

f) Our school has been .... about a forthcoming inspection.

6 marks

Challenge 3

1 Use the clues to complete the words in the grid.

a) To promote a new product, either online, in a magazine or on TV.

b) To cause a device to start working.

c) To attribute human characteristics to something, often a poetic technique.

a)	a							
b)	a							
c)	p							

3 marks

Total: _____ / 15 marks

😐 **Had a go** ☐   🙂 **Getting there** ☐   😄 **Got it!** ☐

Adding the suffix -en to make verbs

Challenge 1

1 Solve the clues to find the verbs.

a) An antonym of tighten

l ....

b) An antonym of bend

s ....

c) An antonym of harden

s ....

d) An antonym of shorten

l ....

e) A synonym for lighten

b ....

f) A synonym for widen

b ....

6 marks

Challenge 2

1 Complete the sentences with a verb made from the words below. Think about the tense that the sentence is in – you may need to make further spelling changes.

| mad | height | sad | moist |

a) Jing was .... when she heard how cruelly the dog had been treated.

b) Ashan took a sip of water to .... his dry throat.

c) The politician said a demonstration would only .... the tension between the two opposing groups.

d) The wicked witch was .... to find she'd been ensnared in a trap!

4 marks

Challenge 3

1 Solve the clues to complete the crossword.

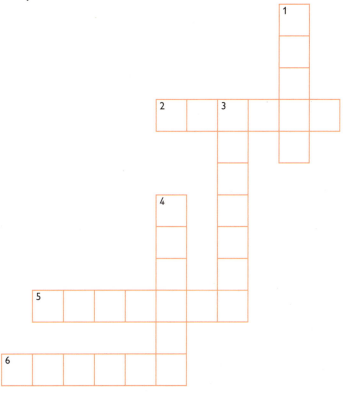

Across

2. To make something happen faster or sooner
5. To crush something
6. To inflame or aggravate a situation

Down

1. To say that a person or thing is similar to another person or thing
3. What you do to a pencil when it's blunt
4. To tidy something up

6 marks

Total: _____ / 16 marks

 Had a go ☐   Getting there ☐   Got it! ☐

Homophones and near-homophones (1)

Homophones are words that sound the same as another word (or words) but have a different meaning and spelling. For example, steak / stake.

Near-homophones are words that sound *almost* the same as another word but have a different meaning and spelling. For example, quiet / quite.

Challenge 1

1 Write a homophone for each word below.

Word	Homophone
board	a)
whose	b)
cannon	c)
creak	d)
soul	e)

5 marks

Challenge 2

1 Write a sentence for each homophone in Challenge 1.

a) ....

b) ....

c) ....

d) ....

e) ....

f) ....

g) ....

h) ....

i) ....

j) ....

20 marks

Challenge 3

1 Match these homophones with their definitions.

| prophet | stationery | addition |
| stationary | edition | profit |

Definition	Word
Not moving	a)
Paper, envelopes and other material	b)
Something added to something	c)
A particular version of a book or magazine	d)
Money gained when you sell something for more than it cost	e)
Someone chosen by God to speak on his behalf	f)

6 marks

Total: _____ / 31 marks

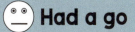

Homophones and near-homophones (2)

Challenge 1

1 Write the correct homophone to complete each sentence.

practice	practise	principals
principles	prophesy	prophecy

a) Jolene likes to .... piano on a Sunday.

b) Our doctor's .... is having an extension.

c) Maya wouldn't do anything that was against her ....

d) There was a meeting of the local schools' ....

e) The .... revealed by the clairvoyant was fulfilled.

f) The detective said he wouldn't like to ....
what would happen if the criminal was not caught.

6 marks

Challenge 2

1 Write a sentence for each of the following near-homophones.

> incite   insight   president
>
> precedent   device   devise

a) ....

b) ....

c) ....

d) ....

e) ....

f) ....

12 marks

Challenge 3

1 Write **two** more homophones for each word below.

a) peak   ....

b) sight   ....

c) basses   ....

d) meat   ....

8 marks

Total: _____ / 26 marks

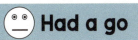 Had a go  Getting there Got it!

61

Words with unspoken sounds and syllables

Challenge 1

1 These words have been written as they are often pronounced – a sound or syllable has been 'lost'. Write them correctly on the lines.

a) parlament ....

b) sevral ....

c) avrage ....

d) marvllous ....

e) cemetry ....

f) dictionry ....

g) intrested ....

h) probly ....

i) evning ....

j) mathmatics ....

10 marks

Challenge 2

1 Use the clues to write words with an unpronounced sound or syllable.

a) An adjective that describes something that is not joined to something else.

s							

b) A group of people who are related to each other.

f					

c) A business or firm that makes money by selling goods or services.

c						

3 marks

Challenge 3

1 Ten words in the passage below have been spelt as they are often said, with an unpronounced syllable or sound. Write the correct spellings on the lines below.

In Febry, Jamil went to his favrite restrant for his twelth birthday. He was accompnied by his parents, his grandparents and his cousin, Amal. Jamil felt privleged to be at the head of the table and smiled happly all through the meal. When they had finished eating, the waiter brought him a choclate cake and they all sang Happy Birthday. Jamil thought it was probly the best evning he'd ever had!

....

....

....

10 marks

Total: _____ / 23 marks

😐 Had a go ☐   🙂 Getting there ☐   😄 Got it! ☐

Dictionary skills (3)

Challenge 1

1   Write these groups of words in alphabetical order.

crafty	linear	unsettled
crack	litter	unreserved
crayon	lipstick	unreasonable
cradle	literal	unruly
cramp	liquid	unqualified
crash	linger	unravel

....

....

....

....

....

....

3 marks

Challenge 2

1   Write four definitions of the word 'squash'. Include the corresponding word class of each.

a)   ....

b) ....

c) ....

d) ....

Challenge 3

1 Look up the following words in your dictionary. Once you have read the definition, write a sentence containing each word.

a) quagmire

....

b) dishevelled

....

c) hullabaloo

....

d) fuchsia

....

e) entourage

....

f) prairie

....

Total: _____ / 19 marks

☺ Had a go ☐   ☺ Getting there ☐   ☺ Got it! ☐

Word games (2)

Challenge 1

1. Find the word in the brackets that is a synonym for the word in bold.
Write the word on the line.

   a) **fierce** (restful   aggressive   bold   tender   direct)

   ....

   b) **dilapidated** (ramshackle   smart   dilated   elegant   final)

   ....

   c) **lessen** (grow   surge   complex   fasten   decrease)

   ....

   3 marks

Challenge 2

1. Write the two words, one from each set of brackets, that are antonyms.

   a) (whisper   secrete   rebel)   (sigh   secret   reveal)

   ....

   b) (interior   sufficient   above)   (superior   within   exterior)

   ....

   c) (altercation   discussion   debate)   (argument   agreement   refusal)

   ....

   3 marks

Challenge 3

1 Fill the grid with the letters below to make four words.

k　　r　　p　　a

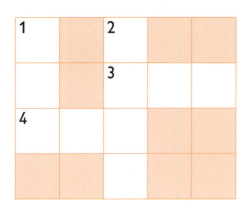

4 marks

2 Fill the grid with the letters below to make seven words.

c　　e　　p　　a　　h

7 marks

Total: _____ / 17 marks

Progress test 3

1. **Find the eight incorrectly spelt words in the passage below.**
   Write the words correctly on the lines.

   It was good to meet Sammie, a news correspondant who is highly proficiant in foreign affairs. Today, she is reporting from a turbulant, war-torn area where there is significant threat to life and an abundance of homeless people. The dominent force is a persistant group, calling themselves Fight for Freedom (FFF), who are being closely monitored by our surveillence team.

   ....

   ....

   ....

   ....

   8 marks

2. **Unscramble these words which all end with a sound like shul.**

   a) **o i m m l e c r c a**   ....

   b) **s u c p e l i i a r f**   ....

   c) **a f a l c i**   ....

   3 marks

3. **Write the answers to the riddles. Use your dictionary to help you with the spelling.**

a) I am a three-syllable adjective; I begin with 'fu' and I mean 'very angry'.

I am ....

b) I am a two-syllable noun; I am a shape which winds round and round, with each curve above or outside the previous one. I can also be a verb or an adjective. I begin with 'sp'.

I am ....

c) I am a five-syllable adjective; I begin with 'aero' and I describe something that moves through the air quickly and easily.

I am ....

3 marks

4. **Select the correct spelling from the pairs of words in bold.**
   Write the correct spelling on the line.

a) When his dad came home early, Raz **seized / siezed** the opportunity to ask for help with his homework.

....

b) According to the geologist, the **glacier / glaceir** appears to have moved further down the mountain.

....

c) Britta kept her **reciept / receipt** in case she changed her mind about her new boots.

....

3 marks

5. Add the suffix -ate, -ise or -ify to each word to make a verb.
Three of the words will need further spelling changes.

a) electric ....

b) moisture ....

c) clear ....

d) scandal ....

e) different ....

f) origin ....

6. Write a definition for each verb you made in Question 5.

a) ....

b) ....

c) ....

d) ....

e) ....

f) ....

7. Write a homophone for each word below.

a) isle ....

b) place ....

c) bread ....

d) chilly ....

e) currant ....

f) maze ....

g) sweet ....

h) gorilla ....

8 marks

8. Find the word in each sentence with a missing apostrophe. Write the words on the lines and add the apostrophes in the correct places.

a) The shoemaker admired the elves neat handiwork.

....

b) We left some money for our waitress tip as she had given us excellent service.

....

c) Eskimos dome-shaped dwellings, which are made from hard snow, are called igloos.

....

3 marks

Total: _____ / 40 marks

Prefixes

Challenge 1

1 One word in each sentence has been given the incorrect prefix.
Write the word correctly on the line.

a) Uwe misapproved of his friend's wild behaviour.

....

b) Chris ilcalculated the distance and drove his car into the wall.

....

c) The fly was able to misentangle itself from the spider's web.

....

d) After many years, Flo inconnected with her long-lost cousins.

....

4 marks

Challenge 2

1 Add a prefix to each word below then complete the sentences. Think about the tense that the sentence is in – you may need to make further spelling changes.

| arm | infect | button | assemble |

a) Tia's wound became .... because she didn't keep it clean.

b) Chai .... his little sister's coat and hung it on the peg.

c) Max had to .... his Lego model after his brother took it apart.

d) It was agreed that the troops would .... and hand in their weapons.

4 marks

Challenge 3

1 Unscramble the letters to find words that start with a prefix that has a negative meaning.

| dapisprvoe ntmisierpret |
| iogalllic bincemala |

....

....

4 marks

Total: _____ / 12 marks

Latin and Greek prefixes

Challenge 1

1 Read the words with prefixes in the box below.
Write the meaning of each prefix on the lines.

antibullying	**co**operate	**sub**-zero
multicoloured	**semi**circle	**inter**national

a) anti ....

b) co ....

c) sub ....

d) multi ....

e) semi ....

f) inter ....

6 marks

74

Challenge 2

1 Add an appropriate prefix to each word then complete the sentences. Think about the tense that the sentence is in – you may need to make further spelling changes.

> attack   function   school   curricular

a) My little sister goes to .... because she is only three.

b) Stuart's computer has .... and he's lost all his data.

c) Rea does musical theatre as an .... activity.

d) The soldiers responded to the enemy with a ....

4 marks

Tip

We use many Latin and Greek prefixes that relate to numbers.
For example, 'mono' (Greek) and 'uni' (Latin) both mean 'one'.

Challenge 3

1 Work out the numerical meaning of each prefix in the words below.
Write the number on the line.

a) **bi**cycle   ....

b) **cent**ury   ....

c) **penta**gon   ....

d) **tri**angle   ....

e) **deca**hedron   ....

f) **quad**rilateral   ....

g) **hex**agon   ....

h) **mille**nnium   ....

8 marks

Total: _____ / 18 marks

 Had a go ☐   **Getting there** ☐   😄 **Got it!** ☐

Words from other languages

1   Write a word that we use in English that contains each of these Latin and Greek roots.
    Use your dictionary to check your spelling.

    a)   alter – other   ....

    b)   chronos – time   ....

    c)   aqua – water   ....

    d)   spectare – look   ....

    e)   phone – sound   ....

    f)   micro – small   ....

    g)   astron – star   ....

    h)   gigas – huge   ....

    i)   phobos – fear   ....

    j)   finis – end   ....

    k)   annus – year   ....

11 marks

Challenge 2

1   Unscramble the letters in bold to complete the sentences with words that have a foreign origin.

a)   Louis doesn't like wearing his school **o r u i f m n**

....

b)   Tim Peake is an **t r a t s n a o u** .... in the European Space Agency.

c)   The singer was having feedback problems with his

i c r m n h o e o p ....

3 marks

Challenge 3

1   Use your dictionary or the internet to find the origin of the words below.
Write each word in the correct place in the table.

| sofa kindergarten bungalow cargo |
| machine blitz shampoo opera picnic |
| avocado barista coffee |

French	Italian
Spanish	**Arabic**
German	**Hindi**

12 marks

Total: _____ / 26 marks

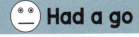 Had a go   Getting there   Got it!

Tricky plurals

Challenge 1

1 Insert the missing plural words to complete each sentence.

| hoof   waterproof   roof   calf   dwarf |

a) On our hike, we walked through a field full of cows and their newborn

....

b) This year's pantomime is a new version of *Snow White and the Seven*

....

c) There was a thundering of .... as the horse race began.

d) A blanket of snow covered the houses' ....

e) We carried our .... in our rucksacks just in case it rained.

5 marks

78

Challenge 2

1 Sort these words according to how their plurals are formed.
Write the plural forms in either group in the table.

diary valley buoy variety play

journey dictionary penny monkey army

-ies endings	-s endings

10 marks

2 Looking at the letter that comes before 'y' in each word, write a spelling rule for making the plural of both groups.

....

....

2 marks

Tip

Words that originate from Latin and Greek don't always follow the normal spelling rules for making plurals. For example, vertex → vertices; fungus → fungi; stadium → stadia; larva → larvae. However, sometimes these words can also just follow the usual rules. For example, vertex → vertexes, stadium → stadiums.

Challenge 3

1 Use the examples in the tip box above to write the plural of each word below.

a) index .... **b)** medium ....

c) radius .... **d)** vertebra ....

4 marks

Total: _____ / 21 marks

😐 **Had a go** ☐   🙂 **Getting there** ☐   😃 **Got it!** ☐

Tricky words (1)

Some words are tricky to spell because they don't follow the spelling or phoneme rules you have learned. Breaking the words into syllables can help you learn to spell them. For example, con-trov-er-sy.

Challenge 1

1. Read each word out loud, then cover, write and check. Use the second line to correct any mistakes or for extra practice.

equipped ....

pronunciation ....

harass ....

variety ....

lightning ....

sincere ....

queue ....

persuade ....

curiosity ....

language ....

thorough ....

sacrifice ....

relevant ....

13 marks

Challenge 2

1   Change the words below into nouns.

persuade   relevant   equipped

....

3 marks

2   Change the words below into adjectives.

curiosity   sacrifice   persuade

....

3 marks

Challenge 3

1   Complete the grid by answering the clues. The answers are words that can be found in Challenge 1, though some have changed their word class. The letters in the shaded squares make another tricky word from Challenge 1. Write the word on the line below.

a)   A verb meaning to annoy or trouble someone.

b)   An adverb meaning done very carefully and in a detailed way.

c)   An adverb meaning you genuinely mean or feel something.

d)   An adjective meaning several different things of a type.

a)

b)

c)

d)

e)   ....

5 marks

Total: _____ / 24 marks

Tricky words (2)

Challenge 1

1   Read each word out loud, then cover, write and check. Use the second line to correct any mistakes or for extra practice.

secretary   ....

parliament   ....

physical   ....

privilege   ....

mischievous   ....

government   ....

ancient   ....

interfere   ....

sufficient   ....

existence   ....

rhyme   ....

familiar   ....

muscle   ....

13 marks

Challenge 2

1 Write the words from Challenge 1 in the correct column in the table below. Some words belong in more than one column.

Noun	Adjective	Verb

17 marks

Challenge 3

1 Complete each sentence with a suitable word from Challenge 1. Think about the tense that the sentence is in – you may need to make further spelling changes.

a) James .... in on my argument with Harry.

b) Recently, we have had a lot of .... from unwanted radio frequency signals.

c) Our old dog is sadly deteriorating .... but he still has his old emotional spark.

d) Gus hoped he had .... money for his bus fare.

4 marks

Total: _____ / 34 marks

 Had a go   **Getting there**   **Got it!**

Dictionary skills (4)

Challenge 1

1 These three words belong to the same word family. Use your dictionary to find the meaning of each.

| circulation | circumspect | circumference |

a) ....

b) ....

c) ....

3 marks

Challenge 2

1 Use your dictionary to find three words that belong in the same family as each root word below.

certain	ascend
office	**break**
press	**process**

18 marks

 Tip A proofreader finds and marks errors that need to be corrected. These might be spelling, punctuation or grammatical mistakes.

1 Proofread the following passage. Write the corrections on the lines below.

 # magazine

Penelope Moneypenny is famus for being opinonated and particularily criticall of the goverment. She is nown for her love of pink lip stick, faux-fur coats and her pink sports car. I cawt up with her in the trendy Café Croissant.

"I'd like to get more envolved in enviromental ishews," she said, flutering her eyelash extentions. "More needs to be done to save are planit. We need to adress climat change much more vigorusly, so I'm traveling in my privat jet next weak to meat members of the Save the World Comittee."

....

....

....

....

....

....

....

....

23 marks

Total: _____ / 44 marks

 Had a go ☐   **Getting there** ☐   ☺ **Got it!** ☐

Word games (3)

Challenge 1

1 Create your own crossword by writing eight more clues where the answers are eight homophones. Use a letter from one word in the answer to form another clue where possible. Shade the squares you don't use. Two have been done for you.

	¹s											
²s	t	a	t	i	o	n	a	r	y			
	a											
	t											
	i											
	o											
	n											
	e											
	r											
	y											

Across

2. Something that is not moving

....

....

....

....

Down

1. Equipment such as paper used for writing

....

....

....

....

8 marks

Challenge 2

1 Write the word that can go in front of each word in the group to make three compound words. One has been done for you.

	side	do	number	*out*
a)	cast	coat	bearing	....
b)	pour	beat	stairs	....
c)	teacher	band	ache	....
d)	some	bag	shake	....

4 marks

> **Tip**
>
> A malapropism is the unintentional use of a word instead of a word with a similar sound. This can often have a humorous effect. For example, Rania was **putrefied** when she saw the large spider, instead of Rania was **petrified** when she saw the large spider.

Challenge 3

1 One word in each sentence has been used incorrectly. Write the correct word on the line.

a) Gina and Mel go flamingo dancing every Saturday morning at the Spanish club.

....

b) Harry was internally grateful to the doctor who operated on his appendix.

....

c) Florence and Bill have a tantrum bicycle which they are taking to the Lake District.

....

d) Felix's gran is an inferior painter and decorator.

....

4 marks

Total: _____ / 16 marks

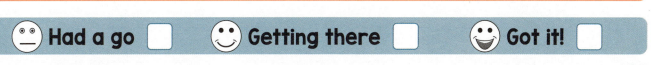

Progress test 4

1. **Add -ify, -ise or -ate to each word below to make verbs. Then use the verbs you have made to complete each sentence. You may need to make additional spelling changes.**

| discrimination | false | special | sympathy |

a) .... b) ....

c) .... d) ....

e) Mel .... with her sister's plight but she was unable to do anything to help her.

f) Terri is always good at .... between a good idea and a bad idea.

g) A woman was arrested earlier today for .... legal documents.

h) Dr McKenzie .... in heart disease.

8 marks

2. **Write these words in alphabetical order.**

| aesthetic | aerodynamic | aeronautic |

....

1 mark

88

3. **Write the word class of each underlined word in the context of the passage in the correct place in the table.**

Despite being fit and underlined healthy, Troy was completely exhausted after his long bike ride with his best friend, Xavier. Having reached their destination, they collapsed breathlessly on the riverbank for a drink and a sandwich. Physical exercise was really important to both boys and they had been planning this ride meticulously for weeks. They had great ambitions of participating in national cycle races but knew they'd have to make a lot of big sacrifices to reach their goal!

Noun	Verb	Adjective	Adverb

16 marks

4. **One word in each sentence is missing its silent letter.**
    Write the words correctly on the lines.

    a) After fishing patiently for over three hours, Maeve finally caught a samon.

    ....

    b) Toni is involved in a legal rangle with his employers so he has decided to engage a solicitor.

    ....

c) As Sven walked glumly towards the headteacher's office, he felt like a condemed man.

....

d) The icicles clung to the fir tree's branches, glisening in the late-night moonlight.

....

5. **One word in each sentence has been given the incorrect prefix. Write the word correctly on the line.**

a) The ball inbounded from the goalpost and hit James squarely in the face.

....

b) Clodagh was misaffected by the new bus timetable as she rides her bike to school.

....

c) Faye uncontinued her piano lessons when she fell in love with the saxophone.

....

6. **Add a prefix to each word below then use the words to complete the grid.**

standard	impose	allow

a) Something that is unacceptable because it is below the required standard.

b) To put an image on top of another image so you can see both images.

c) To reject something because it has been done incorrectly.

a) | | | | | | | | | | |
b) | | | | | | | | | |
c) | | | | | | | |

3 marks

7. **Use the definitions below to complete the answers, which are words that contain an ee sound.**

a) A substance found in food and drink such as meat, nuts and milk that you need to help you grow and be healthy.

p ....

b) A chemical substance found in coffee and tea that makes you more active.

c ....

c) An adjective to describe something that is strange.

w ....

3 marks

Total: _____ / 38 marks

Answers

1. recreate, disrespectful, irrational **[3]**
2. a) There's, who's   b) car's, we'd
   c) Amal's, aren't   d) Let's, I'd **[8]**
3. inference, inferred, interfere, interference **[1]**
4. a) pretentious b) graciously c) fictitious **[3]**
5. a) fasten   b) playwright
   c) undoubtedly **[3]**
6. a) intention   b) procession
   c) deception   d) electrician **[4]**
7. a) paws b) pause c) minute d) minute
   e) hare f) hair **[6]**
8. a) irregular b) misheard c) impractical **[3]**
9. a) league   b) unique   c) antique **[3]**
10. a) discontinue   b) autograph/telegraph
    c) subway   d) antidote **[4]**
11. **Contraction:** couldn't, she'd, who'd, didn't
    Possession: Dad's, year's, Gran's, Anne
    Frank's **[8]**
12. a) initiation   b) condemnation
    c) designation   d) inspiration **[4]**
13. a) denied   b) preferred
    c) permitted   d) buried **[4]**

Challenge 1
1. a) ten | a | cious   b) spa | cious
   c) lus | cious **[6]**
2. a) spacious   b) luscious
   c) tenacious   d) precocious **[4]**
Challenge 2
1. Answers will vary. **[8]**
Challenge 3
1. Answers will vary. **[10]**

Challenge 1
1. a) repetitious   b) nutritious
   c) fictitious   d) contentious **[4]**
Challenge 2
1. a) flirtatious   b) ostentatious
   c) surreptitious   d) conscientious **[4]**
Challenge 3
1. a) pretentious   b) fractious
   c) superstitious   d) scrumptious **[4]**

92

Challenge 1
1. a) sacrificial   b) presidential
   c) torrential   d) prejudicial **[4]**
2. Answers will vary. **[8]**
Challenge 2
1. a) superficial   b) judicial
   c) insubstantial   d) preferential **[4]**
Challenge 3
1. a) confidential   b) potential
   c) consequential. Definitions will
   vary. **[6]**
2. Answers will vary. E.g. Normally, -cial
comes after a vowel but in 'financial' it's a
consonant. Normally, -tial comes after a
consonant but in 'spatial' it's a vowel. **[2]**

Challenge 1
1. a) participant   b) consultant
   c) migrant   d) contaminant **[4]**
Challenge 2
1. relevance, consultancy, radiant, compliance **[4]**
Challenge 3
1. 1. accountancy 2. clairvoyant 3. allegiance
   4. surveillance 5. resistant 6. significance
   7. flamboyant 8. abundant **[8]**

Challenge 1
1. a) efficiency   b) consequence
   c) convenience   d) permanence
   e) persistence   f) turbulence **[6]**
Challenge 2
1. correspondent, existence, precedent,
succulent **[4]**
Challenge 3
1. a) congruent   b) proficiency
   c) resplendent. Sentences will vary. **[9]**

Challenge 1
1. a) unstoppable   b) disreputable
   c) incomprehensible **[3]**

Challenge 2

1. a) pleasurable   b) infallible
    c) certifiable **[3]**

Challenge 3

1. a) rechargeable   b) salvageable
    c) traceable **[3]**
2. a) salvageable   b) rechargeable
    c) traceable **[3]**

Pages 24–25

Challenge 1

1. visibly, abominably, arguably, irresponsibly **[4]**

Challenge 2

1. a) legibly   b) undesirably
    c) feasibly   d) inseparably **[4]**

Challenge 3

1. enviably, forcibly, unjustifiably, inexplicably, incredibly, irreversibly, terribly **[7]**
2. Sentences will vary. **[2]**

Pages 26–27

Challenge 1

1. characterise, oppose, repeat, deceive **[4]**

Challenge 2

1. Answers will vary. **[8]**

Challenge 3

1. Answers will vary. **[2]**
2. boor, noun, someone rude and uneducated; modify, verb, to change something slightly; debris, noun, pieces of rubbish spread about; circumspect, adjective, cautious in what you say or do **[8]**

Pages 28–31

1. a) influential   b) provincial
    c) providential **[3]**
2. a) vice, vicious   b) malice, malicious
    c) space, spacious **[6]**
3. a) incompetence   b) impudence
    c) diligence   d) resurgence **[4]**
4. Answers will vary. **[4]**
5. a) crucial   b) impartial
    c) antisocial. Sentences will vary. **[9]**
6. distinguishable, formidable, inconceivably, questionably, incurable, inexplicably, negotiable, believably **[8]**

Pages 32–33

Challenge 1

1. a) trough   b) plough
    c) brought   d) cough **[4]**

Challenge 2

1. enough, tough; although, dough, though; bought, brought, thought, fought, ought; bough, plough; cough, trough **[14]**

Challenge 3

1. thoroughly, borough. Sentences will vary. **[6]**

Pages 34–35

Challenge 1

1. a) vehemently   b) undoubtedly
    c) gnarled   d) knowledgeably
    e) white   f) rhinoceros **[6]**

Challenge 2

1. a) wedge   b) yolk   c) pneumatic **[3]**

Challenge 3

1. walked, calmly, castle, muscles, columns, aisle, gnarled, well-known, hymn, ghost-like, receipt, answered, aghast, thought **[14]**

Pages 36–37

Challenge 1

1. a) girls'   b) staff's   c) bee's   d) dress's **[4]**

Challenge 2

1. a) bus's   b) Smith's
    c) bosses'   d) children's **[4]**

Challenge 3

1. Kyle's, Bill's, town's, Dad's, weekend's, Dogs' **[6]**

Pages 38–39

Challenge 1

1. How's, What's, I'm, There's, I'll, I've **[6]**

Challenge 2

1. going, wishing, because, having **[4]**

Challenge 3

1. Do you, you would, we have, that is, I am, I would, did not, It is, having, I have, You would, we are, They have, I would, Let us, you have **[16]**

Pages 40–41

Challenge 1

1. light-blue; twenty-three; far-fetched; brand-new **[4]**
2. **First sentence**: the speaker saw a man who was eating shark. **Second sentence**: the speaker saw a shark that eats humans. **[2]**

Challenge 2

1. de-escalate; re-establish/re-escalate; co-author; self-control **[4]**

Challenge 3

1. Answers will vary. **[4]**

Challenge 1

1. **a)** 1 **b)** 2 **c)** 2 **d)** 3 (2 in the suffix plus the 'r' at the start of the word) **[4]**

Challenge 2

1. transferred, transferring; sufferer, suffered, suffering; pilferer, pilfered, pilfering; inferred, inferring **[10]**

Challenge 3

1. 1. suffering 2. transferred 3. referral
4. conferred 5. proffering 6. preferring
7. referendum **[7]**

Challenge 1

1. Answers will vary. **[4]**
2. profession, profound, programme, prophecy **[1]**

Challenge 2

1. Answers will vary. **[4]**

Challenge 3

1. blinking: verb; pebble: noun; fitted: verb; blind: adjective; hopping: verb **[5]**

Challenge 1

1. **a)** hard **b)** shelter
   c) pen **d)** function **[4]**

Challenge 2

1. **a)** instructions **b)** quality
   c) discovered **d)** licensed **[4]**

Challenge 3

1. **a)** wand **b)** tin **c)** man **d)** was **[4]**

1. **a)** kneaded **b)** cologne
   c) fascinated **d)** succumbed **[4]**
2. **a)** thorough **b)** borough
   c) bough **d)** fought **[4]**
3. Answers will vary. **[8]**
4. **a)** journalist's, London's
   b) ladies', town's **c)** dad's, farmers' **[6]**
5. **a)** fair-skinned, blond-haired
   b) free-for-all, empty-handed
   c) twelve-year-old, know-it-all **[6]**
6. **a)** transferred **b)** buffering
   c) deferred **[3]**
7. Answers will vary. E.g. produce: to cause (verb), goods (noun); permit: to allow (verb), licence (noun) **[8]**

8. Can't, I'm, It's, you'd, I've, I'll, Mum's, which'll, Haven't, hotel's, we're, you're **[12]**

Challenge 1

1. protein, weird, seize, caffeine **[4]**
2. Sentences will vary. **[2]**
3. conceited, conceive, deceive, receive **[4]**

Challenge 2

1. **a)** priest **b)** thief **c)** brief **d)** belief **[4]**

Challenge 3

1. briefing, ancient, field, piece, yielded, scientist, believed, seized, shield **[9]**

Challenge 1

1. **a)** vaccinate **b)** agonise **c)** diversify
   d) simplify **e)** validate **f)** equalise **[6]**

Challenge 2

1. **a)** captivated **b)** hospitalised **c)** glorified
   d) hyphenate **e)** fossilised **f)** notified **[6]**

Challenge 3

1. **a)** advertise **b)** activate **c)** personify **[3]**

Challenge 1

1. **a)** loosen **b)** straighten
   c) soften **d)** lengthen
   e) brighten **f)** broaden **[6]**

Challenge 2

1. **a)** saddened **b)** moisten
   c) heighten **d)** maddened **[4]**

Challenge 3

1. 1. liken 2. hasten 3. sharpen 4. neaten
5. flatten 6. worsen **[6]**

Challenge 1

1. **a)** bored **b)** who's **c)** canon
   d) creek **e)** sole **[5]**

Challenge 2

1. Sentences will vary. **[20]**

Challenge 3

1. **a)** stationary **b)** stationery
   c) addition **d)** edition
   e) profit **f)** prophet **[6]**

Challenge 1

1. **a)** practise **b)** practice
   c) principles **d)** principals
   e) prophecy **f)** prophesy **[6]**

Challenge 2
1. Sentences will vary. **[12]**

Challenge 3
1. a) peek, pique   b) cite, site
   c) basis, bases   d) mete, meet **[8]**

Challenge 1
1. a) parliament   b) several   c) average
   d) marvellous   e) cemetery   f) dictionary
   g) interested   h) probably   i) evening
   j) mathematics **[10]**

Challenge 2
1. a) separate   b) family   c) company **[3]**

Challenge 3
1. February, favourite, restaurant, twelfth, accompanied, privileged, happily, chocolate, probably, evening **[10]**

Challenge 1
1. crack, cradle, crafty, cramp, crash, crayon; linear, linger, lipstick, liquid, literal, litter; unqualified, unravel, unreasonable, unreserved, unruly, unsettled **[3]**

Challenge 2
1. Answers will vary. **[4]**

Challenge 3
1. Answers will vary **[12]**

Challenge 1
1. a) aggressive b) ramshackle c) decrease **[3]**

Challenge 2
1. a) secrete, reveal   b) interior, exterior
   c) altercation, agreement **[3]**

Challenge 3
1. 1. rap   2. park   3. ark   4. par **[4]**
2. 1. peach (across), pea (down) 2. ape 3. ace
   4. cape 5. pace 6. cap **[7]**

1. correspondent, proficient, turbulent, significant, abundance, dominant, persistent, surveillance **[8]**
2. a) commercial   b) superficial
   c) facial **[3]**
3. a) furious   b) spiral
   c) aerodynamic **[3]**
4. a) seized   b) glacier   c) receipt **[3]**

5. a) electrify   b) moisturise
   c) clarify   d) scandalise
   e) differentiate   f) originate **[6]**
6. Answers will vary. **[6]**
7. a) aisle b) plaice c) bred   d) chilli
   e) current   f) maize   g) suite
   h) guerrilla **[8]**
8. a) elves'   b) waitress's   c) Eskimos' **[3]**

Challenge 1
1. a) disapproved   b) miscalculated
   c) disentangle   d) reconnected **[4]**

Challenge 2
1. a) reinfected   b) unbuttoned
   c) reassemble   d) disarm **[4]**

Challenge 3
1. disapprove, misinterpret, illogical, imbalance **[4]**

Challenge 1
1. a) against   b) together/with
   c) under/below   d) many
   e) half   f) between/among **[6]**

Challenge 2
1. a) preschool   b) malfunctioned
   c) extracurricular d) counterattack **[4]**

Challenge 3
1. a) two   b) hundred   c) five   d) three
   e) ten   f) four   g) six
   h) thousand **[8]**

Challenge 1
1. Answers will vary. **[11]**

Challenge 2
1. a) uniform   b) astronaut
   c) microphone **[3]**

Challenge 3
1. **French:** machine, picnic **Italian:** opera, barista **Spanish:** cargo, avocado **Arabic:** sofa, coffee **German:** kindergarten, blitz **Hindi:** bungalow, shampoo **[12]**

Challenge 1
1. a) calves   b) Dwarves / Dwarfs
   c) hoofs / hooves   d) roofs
   e) waterproofs **[5]**

Challenge 2

1. **-ies endings:** diaries, varieties, dictionaries, pennies, armies **-s endings:** valleys, buoys, plays, journeys, monkeys **[10]**
2. Answers will vary. E.g. If there's a consonant before a final 'y', change the 'y' to 'ie' and add 's'. If there's a vowel before a final 'y', just add 's'. **[2]**

Challenge 3

1. **a)** indices / indexes **b)** media / mediums
    c) radii **d)** vertebrae **[4]**

Pages 80–81

Challenge 1

1. Words spelt correctly **[13]**

Challenge 2

1. persuasion, relevance, equipment **[3]**
2. curious, sacrificial, persuasive **[3]**

Challenge 3

1. **a)** harass **b)** thoroughly
    c) sincerely **d)** various
    e) relevant **[5]**

Pages 82–83

Challenge 1

1. Words spelt correctly. **[13]**

Challenge 2

1. **Noun:** secretary, parliament, physical, privilege, government, existence, rhyme, muscle **Adjective:** physical, mischievous, ancient, sufficient, familiar **Verb:** privilege, interfere, rhyme, muscle **[17]**

Challenge 3

1. **a)** muscled / muscles **b)** interference
    c) physically **d)** sufficient **[4]**

Pages 84–85

Challenge 1

1. Answers will vary. **[3]**

Challenge 2

1. Answers will vary. **[18]**

Challenge 3

1. famous, opinionated, particularly, critical, government, known, lipstick, caught, involved, environmental, issues, fluttering, extensions, our, planet, address, climate, vigorously, travelling, private, week, meet, Committee **[23]**

Pages 86–87

Challenge 1

1. Answers will vary. **[8]**

Challenge 2

1. **a)** over **b)** down
    c) head **d)** hand **[4]**

Challenge 3

1. **a)** flamingo – flamenco
    b) internally – eternally
    c) tantrum – tandem
    d) inferior – interior **[4]**

Pages 88–91

1. **a)** discriminate **b)** falsify
    c) specialise **d)** sympathise
    e) sympathised **f)** discriminating
    g) falsifying
    h) specialises / specialised **[8]**
2. aerodynamic, aeronautic, aesthetic **[1]**
3. **Noun:** ride, riverbank, exercise, ambitions
    Verb: reached, planning, had, make
    Adjective: healthy, best, important, national
    Adverb: completely, breathlessly, really, meticulously **[16]**
4. **a)** salmon **b)** wrangle
    c) condemned **d)** glistening **[4]**
5. **a)** rebounded **b)** unaffected
    c) discontinued **[3]**
6. **a)** substandard **b)** superimpose
    c) disallow **[3]**
7. **a)** protein **b)** caffeine **c)** weird **[3]**